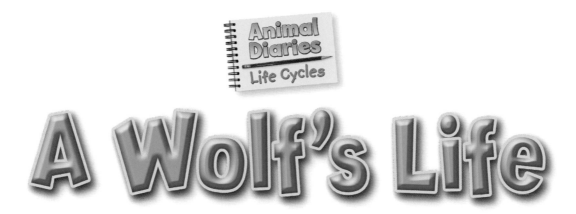

A Wolf's Life

by Ellen Lawrence

Consultants:

Erin Hunt
General Manager, California Wolf Center, Julian, California

Kimberly Brenneman, PhD
National Institute for Early Education Research, Rutgers University, New Brunswick, New Jersey

BEARPORT
PUBLISHING

New York, New York

Credits

Cover, © © Kurt Möbus/Imagebroker/FLPA and © B.G. Smith/Shutterstock and © Jurgen & Christine Sohns/FLPA; 2–3, © Cynthia Kidwell/Shutterstock; 4T, © Max Topchii/Shutterstock; 4B, © Cosmographics; 5, © Herbert Kehrer/Imagebroker/ FLPA; 6, © Michael Weber/Imagebroker/FLPA; 6–7C, © Cynthia Kidwell/Shutterstock; 7, © David Tipling/FLPA; 8, © Minden Pictures/Superstock; 9, © Don Enger/Animals Animals; 10, Daniel J. Cox/Getty Images; 11, © Jim Brandenburg/Minden Pictures/FLPA; 12–13, © Stan Tekiela/Nature Smart Wildlife Images; 14, © A. von Dueren/Shutterstock; 15TL, © Imagebroker/ FLPA; 15, © Imagebroker/FLPA; 16, © Imagebroker/FLPA; 16–17, © Imagebroker/FLPA; 18T, © Richard Seeley/Shutterstock; 18B, © Melissa Schalke/Shutterstock; 19, © David Tipling/FLPA; 20, © Wollertz/Shutterstock; 21, © Jörn Friederich/ Imagebroker/FLPA; 22, © Eric Milos/Shutterstock and © James Pierce/Shutterstock and © pandapaw/Shutterstock; 23TL, © Michael Weber/Imagebroker/FLPA; 23TC, © Don Enger/Animals Animals; 23TR, © Denis Pepin/Shutterstock; 23BL, © Torsten Lorenz/Shutterstock; 23BC, © Pictureguy/Shutterstock; 23BR, © Carol Heesen/Shutterstock.

Publisher: Kenn Goin
Senior Editor: Lisa Wiseman
Creative Director: Spencer Brinker
Design: Alix Wood
Editor: Mark J. Sachner
Photo Researcher: Ruby Tuesday Books Ltd

Library of Congress Cataloging-in-Publication Data

Lawrence, Ellen, 1967–
  A wolf's life / by Ellen Lawrence.
      p. cm. — (Animal diaries : life cycles)
  Includes bibliographical references and index.
  ISBN 978-1-61772-597-5 (library binding) — ISBN 1-61772-597-8 (library binding)
  1. Wolves—Life cycles—Juvenile literature. I. Title.
  QL737.C22L336 2013
  599.773139—dc23
                        2012014768

For more information, write to Bearport Publishing Company, Inc., 45 West 21st Street, Suite 3B, New York, New York 10010. Printed in the United States of America.

10 9 8 7 6 5 4 3 2 1

Contents

Name: **Maddie**   Date: **February 15**

Wolf Watching

Today, I watched a **pack** of gray wolves.

I was in the forest with my mom.

She is a scientist who studies wolves.

Wolves live in mountains, thick forests, and sometimes in areas of flat land covered with grass called prairies.

They are afraid of people, so they make their homes far from towns and cities.

Maddie

Mom

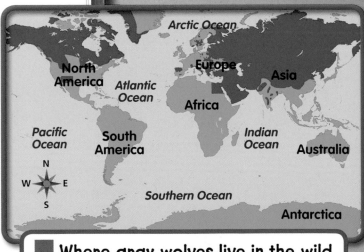

Arctic Ocean

North America   Europe   Asia

Atlantic Ocean

Africa

Pacific Ocean   South America   Indian Ocean   Australia

N
W   E
S

Southern Ocean

Antarctica

■ Where gray wolves live in the wild

gray wolf

Wolves belong to the same animal family as coyotes, foxes, and pet dogs.

Draw a wolf on a piece of paper. Then label different parts of its body. Use these words to help you.

ears

tail

thick fur

nose

5

Date: **February 28**

Life in the Pack

The wolf pack that my mom studies has eight members.

The pack is led by a male and a female, called the **alpha wolves**.

They are the mother and father of the other pack members.

This evening we watched and listened as the wolf pack howled together.

My mom said the wolves were telling each other, "It's time to go hunting!"

alpha female

alpha male

Scientists think wolves howl for many reasons. One reason is to let other pack members know where they are. Another reason is to warn other packs to stay out of their **territory**.

Date: April 15

Digging a Den

My mom says the alpha wolves **mated** in February, about eight weeks ago.

Now, it is nearly time for the female wolf to give birth to her pups, or cubs.

That's why the female began to dig a big hole today.

The hole is the entrance to her underground **den,** which is like a small cave.

The den is where she will give birth to her pups.

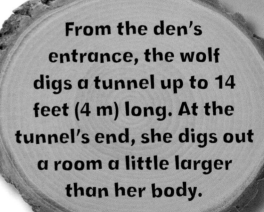

female wolf digging

From the den's entrance, the wolf digs a tunnel up to 14 feet (4 m) long. At the tunnel's end, she digs out a room a little larger than her body.

female wolf

entrance to den

9

Date: **April 25**

The Pups Are Here!

It has been three days since the female wolf went into her den.

We haven't seen her since—which means she has given birth to her pups.

For a few weeks after they are born, the tiny pups cannot walk or hear.

Their eyes are closed.

To get food, they drink milk from their mother's body.

They snuggle into her fur to stay warm.

For three weeks the mother wolf hardly ever leaves her tiny babies alone.

mother wolf in den

wolf pup

During the time when the mother cannot leave the pups, she may get hungry. How do you think she gets food?

Date: **May 13**

Life in the Den

It's been almost three weeks since the pups were born.

Their eyes are now open, and they can also walk and hear.

The pups spend their time exploring and playing inside the den.

Since the mother cannot leave the pups, other pack members bring meat for her to eat.

Bringing food to each other is one way that wolf families take care of the members of their pack.

mother wolf

pup

13

Date: **May 20**

The Pups Leave the Den

Today, six little pups came outside the den for the first time!

The pups still drink their mother's milk, but we saw them try some meat, too.

The pups licked around their father's mouth to tell him they were hungry.

So he spat up some chewed-up meat for them to try!

That's how wolf pups get their first taste of meat.

den

pups outside den

A mother wolf usually gives birth to four to seven pups. Sometimes, however, she can give birth to as many as 14.

mother wolf

father wolf

pups drinking milk

pup asking for meat

15

Wolf Pup Games

The pups are now almost ten weeks old.

They no longer live in the den.

They spend their days and nights out in the forest with the older wolves.

When the pack goes hunting, one wolf stays behind and babysits the playful pups.

The little wolves spend their time chasing one another and play fighting.

wolf pup

adult babysitter wolf

Wolf pups stop drinking milk and eat only meat when they are about eight weeks old. At that time, all the pack members start to bring the pups meat to eat.

ten-week-old
wolf pup

How do you think
chasing one another
will help the pups
when they are adults?

17

Date: **December 15**

Going On a Hunt

The wolf pups are now about eight months old, and have started hunting with the pack!

Wolves hunt large **prey** such as moose, deer, bison, elk, and reindeer.

The pack uses teamwork to catch these big, fast animals.

For example, the wolves may take turns chasing an animal to make it tired.

moose

bison

Date: **January 15**

Growing Up

The young wolves are now nine months old.

They will live with their parents' pack for around two more years.

When their mother has new pups, they will babysit for their little brothers and sisters.

When the young wolves are two to three years old, most of them will go off on their own.

One day, some of the wolves may have the chance to be alpha wolves in their own packs.

nine-month-old wolf

Wolf packs usually have between five and nine members. A large pack can have around 30 members!

How is a wolf family
like your family?
How is it different?

Science Lab

Be a wolf scientist

Scientists sometimes find wolves by following their tracks, or footprints, in snow or on muddy ground.

Wolf tracks can tell scientists where the wolves are living and what they do.

Follow the wolf tracks on the map and then answer these questions.

1) Where did the wolves walk to first? Why do you think they went to this place?

2) Which animal did the wolves hunt?

3) Wolves sometimes have more than one den. Which den are the wolves using today? What clues can you see that tell you where the wolves are living? Use the map key to help you.

(The answers are on page 24.)

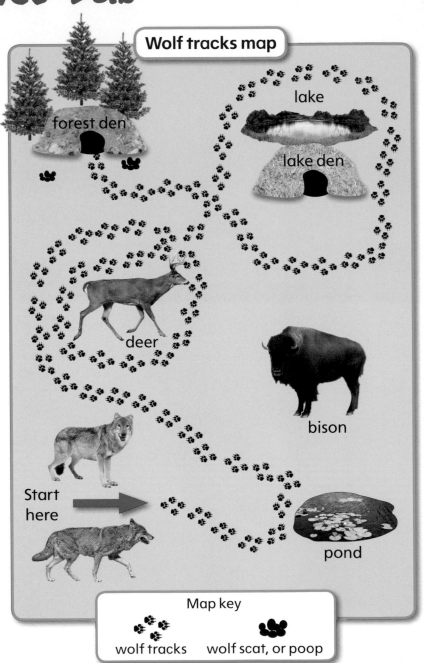

Wolf tracks map

lake

forest den

lake den

deer

bison

Start here

pond

Map key

wolf tracks   wolf scat, or poop

Science Words

alpha wolves (AL-fuh WULVZ) the two highest-ranked wolves, a male and a female, in a pack

den (DEN) a home where animals can rest, be safe, and have babies

mated (MATE-id) came together to have young

pack (PAK) a group of wolves that live together

prey (PRAY) animals hunted by other animals

territory (TER-uh-tor-ee) an area of land that belongs to an animal

Index

Read More

Barrett, Jalma. *Wolf (Wild Canines of North America).* Woodbridge, CT: Blackbirch (2000).

Kalman, Bobbie, and Amanda Bishop. *The Life Cycle of a Wolf (The Life Cycles Series).* New York: Crabtree (2002).

Markle, Sandra. *Family Pack.* Watertown, MA: Charlesbridge (2011).

Learn More Online

To learn more about wolves, visit **www.bearportpublishing.com/AnimalDiaries**

Answers

Here are the answers to the questions on page 22.

1) The wolves went to the pond first to drink some water.
2) The wolves hunted a deer.
3) The wolves are using the forest den. There is wolf scat and some wolf tracks outside the den. These clues show a scientist there are wolves at home!

About the Author

Ellen Lawrence lives in the United Kingdom. Her favorite books to write are those about animals. In fact, the first book Ellen bought for herself, when she was six years old, was the story of a gorilla named Patty Cake that was born in New York's Central Park Zoo.